Keep 'Em Rolling, Andy Capp

by
Smythe

A FAWCETT GOLD MEDAL BOOK

Fawcett Publications, Inc., Greenwich, Connecticut

KEEP 'EM ROLLING, ANDY CAPP

ANDY CAPP of the Daily Mirror, London

Copyright © IPC Newspaper Ltd. 1973.

Copyright © 1975 by Fawcett Publications, Inc.

Copyright under International and Pan-American Copyright Conventions

Published by special arrangement with Field Newspaper Syndicate

Printed in the United States of America

2   3   4   5   6   7   8   9   10

OH DEAR, DEAR! LOST YER VOICE, KID?

RUBY! WHEN YOU'VE GOT THROUGH WITH CHALKIE, CAN YER COME AN' TAKE OVER?!

5-10-73

WILL YOU JOIN ME IN A BRANDY, MOTHER?

VERY KIND OF YER, FLO

5-23-73

HEY! THAT BRANDY'S ONLY T' BE USED IN AN EMERGENCY!

MARRIED TO YOU, MATEY, EVERYTHIN'S AN EMERGENCY!

Smythe

8-9-73

8·15·73

8-27-73

9-4-73

9-6-73

THERE WAS ANOTHER SHOP WINDOW BROKEN DOWN THE ROAD LAS'NIGHT — FLIPPIN' HOOLIGANS! THEY SHOULD BRING BACK CONSCRIPTION!!

...MIND YOU, 'E WAS IN THE ARMY F' YEARS...

9-10-73

ON SECOND THOUGHTS, MEBBE THEY SHOULDN'T

9-12-73

9-17-73

WHAT WAS ALL THE COMMOTION?

THIS IS THE ONLY DUMP IN THE WORLD YOU CAN BE 'OMESICK FOR WHILE YOU'RE STILL IN IT!

EMPLOYMENT
EXCHANGE

10-24-73

-HIC-

...IT'S ONE OF
LIFE'S LITTLE
MYSTERIES —

'E MANAGES TO LIVE IT UP
EVEN THOUGH 'E RECKONS
'E CAN'T EXIST ON THE
WAGES 'E TURNS DOWN!

HUH! SOME DATE! SOME MANNERS!

SORRY, DARLIN' —

'ERE YOU ARE — YOU CAN 'AVE THE CENTRE PAGE

10-30-73

THE POOR LASS 'AS TO WORK VERY 'ARD TO GET THAT MONEY, MATE...

SO WHY GIVE 'ER THE FURTHER 'ARDSHIP OF TRYIN' T' SAVE IT?

Smythe

WHY DON'T YOU TALK TO ME WHILE I'M KNITTIN'?

I'VE GOT A BETTER IDEA—

YOU KNIT TO ME WHILE I'M WATCHIN' TELLY

Smythe

ACCEPT YER FATE, LAD, YOU'LL NEVER BE RICH, YOU'RE LIVIN' IN THE WRONG PLACE IN THE WRONG TIME....

11-12-73

EVERYTHIN'S ALREADY BEEN DONE AROUND THESE PARTS, EVERYTHIN'S BEEN THOUGHT OF...

FLO, IS THERE ANY UNDERDEVELOPED TERRITORY NOT FAR FROM 'ERE?

YES...ER... I MEAN, NO

I MEAN YES! — UNDER YER FLIPPIN' CAP, MATE!

Smythe

I'M GOIN' DOWN T' THE MARKET. C'MON, PET, GIVE ME A HAND WITH THE SHOPPIN' — IT WON'T 'URT YOU TO MISS THE RACIN' F' ONCE

11-13-73

I DON'T THINK YOU 'AVE ANY CONCEPTION OF THE WORK THAT GOES INTO THESE OUTSIDE BROADCASTS—!

'OW DO YOU THINK THEY'D FEEL IF THEY THOUGHT THAT NOBODY WAS WATCHIN'?!

I SHOULD BE ASHAMED OF MESELF

REMEMBER NOW, I DON'T WANT THE PERFORMANCE WE 'AD LAS' NIGHT WHEN YOU CAME 'OME—

11-14-73

WAKIN' UP THE WHOLE STREET WITH THEM INSULTIN' FOLK SONGS!

FOLK SONGS—?

YES! —MY FOLKS!!

11-16-73

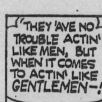

Fawcett Gold Medal Books
in the Andy Capp Series
by Smythe

ANDY CAPP, MAN OF THE HOUR	13593-4	$1.25
ANDY CAPP SOUNDS OFF	M3397	95¢
ANDY CAPP STRIKES BACK (abridged)	M3390	95¢
ANDY CAPP, THE ONE AND ONLY	13684-1	$1.25
HARD AT WORK, ANDY CAPP?	13725-2	$1.25
HATS OFF, ANDY CAPP	13769-4	$1.25
HURRAY FOR ANDY CAPP (abridged)	P3550	$1.25
IN YOUR EYE, ANDY CAPP (abridged)	13590-X	$1.25
IT'S PUB TIME, ANDY CAPP	13609-4	$1.25
KEEP 'EM ROLLING, ANDY CAPP	1-3841-0	$1.25
LIVE IT UP, ANDY CAPP	P3565	$1.25
MEET ANDY CAPP	13716-3	$1.25
NONE OF YOUR LIP, ANDY CAPP!	13719-8	$1.25
RISE AND SHINE, ANDY CAPP!	13708-2	$1.25
TAKE A BOW, ANDY CAPP	13629-9	$1.25
THE UNDISPUTED ANDY CAPP	13668-X	$1.25
VERY SNEAKY, ANDY CAPP	13627-2	$1.25
WATCH YOUR STEP, ANDY CAPP	P3562	$1.25
WHAT NEXT, ANDY CAPP	13628-0	$1.25
YOU'RE A RIOT, ANDY CAPP	13591-8	$1.25
YOU'RE SOME HERO, ANDY CAPP	P3561	$1.25
YOU TELL 'EM, ANDY CAPP	13594-2	$1.25
YOU'RE THE BOSS, ANDY CAPP	13631-0	$1.25